To my Grand
Lily. Gram
loves you
and I am so
proud of you.

MW00647965

$\mathcal{A}$ granddaughter is love
and everything beautiful

♡ Susan Polis Schutz

Copyright © 2021, 2022 by Blue Mountain Arts, Inc.

All rights reserved. No part of this publication may be reproduced, stored in a retrieval system or transmitted in any form or by any means, electronic, mechanical, photocopying, recording or otherwise, without the written permission of the publisher.

We wish to thank Susan Polis Schutz for permission to reprint the following poems that appear in this publication: "A granddaughter is love…," "I remember…," "Granddaughter…," and "I am so happy with the direction…." Copyright © 1987, 1988, 2004, 2016 by Stephen Schutz and Susan Polis Schutz. All rights reserved.

ISBN: 978-1-68088-428-9 (previously ISBN: 978-1-68088-357-2)

◗◖ and Blue Mountain Press are registered in U.S. Patent and Trademark Office. Certain trademarks are used under license.

Acknowledgments appear on the last page.

Printed in China.
First printing of this edition: 2022

✪ This book is printed on recycled paper.

This book is printed on paper that has been specially produced to be acid free (neutral pH) and contains no groundwood or unbleached pulp. It conforms with the requirements of the American National Standards Institute, Inc., so as to ensure that this book will last and be enjoyed by future generations.

Blue Mountain Arts, Inc.
P.O. Box 4549, Boulder, Colorado 80306

A Granddaughter Is Love

A Blue Mountain Arts® Collection

Edited by Patricia Wayant
and Becky McKay

Blue Mountain Press™
Boulder, Colorado

A
Granddaughter
Is Love

Granddaughter,
you have been a delight since
    the day you were born,
and I'm continually thankful
    for the joy you bring to me.

Your smiles still light up my life.
Your accomplishments make me proud.

Your laughter still makes me feel
    like everything is good and right,
and that as long as you're happy
    the world has hope for the future.

Always remember that you are
precious and unique;
there's no one in this world
who could ever take your place.

♡ Barbara Cage

I Am So Blessed
to Be a Part of Your Life

Just calling you my granddaughter makes me smile. Ever since you came into this world, you have brought me so much joy that I can't even remember what my life was like before. Everything you do makes me proud — you've always been such an enthusiastic achiever, eager to try new challenges. But it's the time we share together as grandparent and grandchild that brings me the most happiness.

I love to share my past and present experiences and thoughts about the future with someone who truly cares and listens with interest. My heart longs to see you become an important part of the future because you are so smart, ambitious, and caring with so much to offer the world.

Your love embraces my heart every moment we share together. You are so beautiful inside and out, and you will always be so special to me. I'm so proud to call you my granddaughter, and I'll always love you.

♡ Dianne Cogar

When You Were Little...

I remember
rock, rock, rocking
all my love
into the beautiful miracle
that was you as a baby
hugging you so close
hoping my arms would
protect you from all
struggles
Rock, rock, rocking
as I gazed at this new life
that was you
kissing your little head
hoping that you would always be
as peaceful as you were then

♡ Susan Polis Schutz

If my memories were photographs, some would show you, held as a baby in the warmth of my arms, with me looking as proud as anyone could ever be. And they would show you, as you grew, celebrating the special days of your life on through the years…

I don't think anything can bring such joyful tears to my eyes as my thoughts of you can. And I want you to know that each one of those tears is filled with happiness and gratitude and a prayer for something I wish you knew:

Granddaughters are some of the sweetest people in the world. And I'll always thank God that the sweetest of all… turned out to be you.

♡ Laurel Atherton

Know That
You Are Loved

Don't ever forget that you are unique.
Be your best self
and not an imitation of someone else.
Find your strengths
and use them in a positive way.
Don't listen to those
who ridicule the choices you make.
Travel the road that you have chosen
and don't look back with regret.
You have to take chances
to make your dreams happen.
Remember that there is plenty of time
to travel another road —
    and still another —
in your journey through life.
Take the time to find the route
that is right for you.
You will learn something valuable
from every trip you take,
so don't be afraid to make mistakes.

Tell yourself that you're okay
just the way you are.
Make friends who respect your true self.
Take the time to be alone, too,
so you can know just how terrific
your own company can be.
Remember that being alone
doesn't always mean being lonely;
it can be a beautiful experience
of finding your creativity,
your heartfelt feelings,
and the calm and quiet peace
      deep inside you.

Please don't ever forget
that you are special
and very much loved.

♡ Jacqueline Schiff

You Bring So Much Sunshine into My Life

Every time we get to see each other,
I am delighted as can be.
Watching you grow and blossom
into a lovely young woman
has been one of the greatest blessings
    of my life.
You look at the world with such
    enthusiastic wonder
that I also start seeing my surroundings
with a fresh and new perspective.

Don't ever lose your sense of optimism,
your natural curiosity, and your
    enthusiasm for life.
You have the natural ability
to bring joy to even the most steadfast cynic.
These are just a few of the thousands of things
I cherish about you.

♡ Betsy Logan

Granddaughter
you are such a delight
such a joy
such a beautiful person
The love I see in your eyes for me
is so moving and rewarding
and I hope you see and feel
the infinite love I have for you
Whatever you do
wherever you go
always know that
I am always here
in every way
for you
— Susan Polis Schutz

Don't Ever Lose Sight of Who You Are

Don't ever lose sight of the gift that is you. When life seems to knock you down, get back up and get back in the game. Remember what you're made of. Remember what's flowing in your veins. Remember what you were given, and remember what you went out and created on your own. Like any great masterpiece, you're not done yet. Inside you is the best of everyone who has come before you — and the best of everyone yet to be. You can forget some of what life hands you, but never ever forget who you are.

♡ Rachel Snyder

$\mathcal{E}$very day, remind yourself of all the things you are good at and all that you are capable of accomplishing in every area of your life. You are amazing in every way, and you should always remember that! Don't let other people discourage you from reaching for your dreams. What you do is up to you, because you are the only one who knows what you are capable of.

Envision yourself succeeding. Imagine what you are going to accomplish, and then take the steps to actually achieve what you want to do. Don't let any missteps discourage you in any way. Focus on the future and all you can do to make it unforgettable. You are irreplaceable and incredible, and there is no one else like you.

♡ Ashley Rice

Have Faith in Yourself...

Sometimes the world
tries to steer you
in strange directions.
It tries to mold you into
something you're not,
and you start down paths
you never intended to take.

That's when you need to stop
and focus on who you are
and what you stand for.
When you do, your light will shine and
the world will see the power within you —
and you will too.

Stay true to yourself
and your values,
and have faith in yourself.

♡ Suzy Toronto

When I was young, my grandmother told my sisters and me that we each had our own star in the sky. *How do I tell which star is mine?* I asked her. *It's the one that shines the brightest to you*, said my grandmother. No matter what you call your inner voice, or what form it takes — your star, your guardian angel, your creator, your God, your highest self — it is always looking out for you.

Your inner voice is always there to remind you that you are not alone. Its goal isn't to ensure we play it safe or never have fun. Sometimes, in fact, it pushes us to take risks. These days, before I make any decision, I check in with my inner voice. It needs to signal to me a quiet *Yes, this is the right thing to do*, before I move forward.

♡ Gisele Bündchen

...and Always Follow Your Heart

Always remember to live your life
   in a way that's right for you.
Everything you do should make you happy,
and those who may at first disagree
   will hopefully, in time,
      be happy for you too.
Then you will come to see
      that the choices you make are right —
         if you make them for yourself.

♡ Jodi R. Ernst

Go where the heart
longs to go
Don't pay attention to the feet
that want to stay rooted

Go where the mind
wants to explore
Don't worry about the hands
that still want to hold on

Go where your gut
is fearful to go
Don't let your body
sit in one place

Go where your heart
knows it should go

♡ Natasha Josefowitz

So long as you are true to the strength within your
own heart… you can never go wrong.

♡ Ashley Rice

A Granddaughter Is...

...one of life's
most beautiful blessings.

♡ Laurel Atherton

...a beautiful reflection of yesterday,
a joyful promise of tomorrow.

♡ Author Unknown

...someone who makes everything a
lot more lovely... and a little more of
a miracle... everywhere she goes.

♡ Chris Gallatin

...a priceless reminder of all that is good and
right in this world.

♡ Lily Fisher Doggett

...the inspiration for more smiles than I will ever be able to count, the sunshine in my days, the princess of my heart, and the sweetest gift this world has ever known.

♡ Douglas Pagels

...a precious miracle who stole my heart the moment she was born and has been in possession of it ever since.

♡ Anna Marie Edwards

...love and everything beautiful

♡ Susan Polis Schutz

There Is So Much Potential Inside of You

You have so much to offer,
so much to give, and
so much you deserve
to receive in return.
Don't ever doubt that.

Know yourself and all your fine
    qualities.
Rejoice in all your marvelous strengths
    of mind and body.
Be glad for the virtues that are yours,
    and pat yourself on the back for all
    your many admirable achievements.

Keep positive.
Concentrate on that which
    makes you happy,
        and build yourself up.
Stay nimble of heart,
    happy of thought,
    healthy of mind, and
        well in being.

♡ Janet A. Sullivan-Bradford

There is inside you
all of the potential to be whatever
    you want to be —
all of the energy to do whatever
    you want to do.
Imagine yourself as you would like to be,
    doing what you want to do,
and each day, take one step
    toward your dream.

♡ Donna Levine-Small

When Life Is Hard, Granddaughter, Don't Give Up

Sometimes we don't know our power until the time comes to use it. It lies dormant within us and emerges just when we think we can't go on. And when it does, we find that we had much more power and strength than we ever thought possible.

So when you feel like giving up and throwing in the towel, know in your heart that your strength is on its way to the surface. One day you will look back and see just how strong you really were.

♡ Lamisha Serf-Walls

Do Not Lose Faith in People

I wish I could say everyone will like you and love you. And most will. A few will not and you won't know why. Don't spend time feeling bad about it — wish them your best and go be with those who want your star to shine.

What I can't tell you is why bad things happen, things that may upset or scare you, mean things that people do to one another. You won't understand why, and I can't explain it. No one really can. Because no one really knows.

You must not lose faith in people. Some will explain things according to their beliefs. Do not simply accept their beliefs. Question everything and seek answers. Seek your own truth.

Look for the good in people and you'll find it. When you do, let it rub off on you. When you see the bad in people, try to help them to see the good in themselves. Give them a second chance. Don't hate when you see people hurt one another. Be kind, be empathetic, but be strong in your conviction to stand up for what is good in this world. There is so much good!

♡ Lois Paige Simenson

Family and Friends Will Always Be There for You

Family is a feeling of
belonging and acceptance.
It's a safe retreat, a shelter,
and an instant connection
to the people who have faith in you.
It's a special source of well-being —
full of people who hold you
    in the roughest times,
share your life,
and love to be there for you.

♡ Barbara J. Hall

Our friends are always there to
shine upon our triumphs,
guide us through darkness,
and show us we are never alone.
They give beauty to our lives,
inspiration to our souls, and
peace to our hearts.

♡ Katie Newell

My Granddaughter, Look for Reasons to Laugh and Be Joyful

I think one of the most important things in life is to laugh as much as possible. I confess that, as of late, it is sometimes difficult for me to find humor in the world. I am not alone in this respect: I believe that far too many have lost a sense of humor, largely because the world seems too complicated and dominated by uncontrollable forces. That perspective, however, misconstrues the true source of joy.

Happiness and joy lie inside of us, not in the external world. To think that one can only be happy if the external conditions are ripe leads only to disappointment. Guffaws require but a flimsy excuse to escape, and embracing the absurd is the most fertile environment for laughter. So, when the world seems a little gloomy, just tilt your head a little bit and see the world slightly askew. I will work harder to follow my own advice.

♡ Vinnie Ferraro

Once in a very great while, more often if you're incredibly lucky, joy will drop into your life. It may be a simple thing, such as seeing an exceptionally beautiful flower, or it might be one of life's peak experiences, like the birth of a child, that triggers the emotion of joy. Whatever brings it on, take immediate action. Notice it, stop everything else. Breathe it in, listen to it, touch it, taste it, smell it, revel in it, roll around in it, suspend time, and ignore everyone else. This is too important for manners, for civilized, polite behavior. Joy is elemental, real, and rare.

♡ Linda Abbott Trapp

What I Want for You

Happiness that shines on you along every path you walk
Faith to guide you so you never feel lost
Hope to keep you positive and strong
Peace — so you can hear the songs that sing in your heart
Sunshine to dry any tears
Courage to stick to your principles
Respect for your feelings, needs, and dreams
Laughter wherever your spirit travels
Family connections that nurture, protect, encourage, and
    help you flourish as an individual
Adventures that widen your horizons
Love that comes with all these other wishes that are in
    my heart for you

♡ Jacqueline Schiff

I want you to know how amazing you are.
I want you to know how much you're
treasured and celebrated and quietly thanked.
I want you to feel really good...
    about who you are.
About all the great things you do!
I want you to appreciate your uniqueness.
Acknowledge your talents
    and abilities.
Realize what a beautiful soul you have.
Understand the wonder within.
You are a very special person,
giving so many people a reason to smile.
You deserve to receive the best in return,
and one of my heart's favorite hopes is that
the happiness you give away will come back
to warm you each and every day
    of your life.

♡ Sydney Nealson

Thank You, Granddaughter

You've added so much joy to my life.
Though we come from different generations,
our hearts share the same laughter
and the same love.
Those are two things in life
that age cannot change.

If I could tell you a million times a day
that I love you — and hug you just as much —
that still would never be enough
to express just how much you mean to me.
I hope you are reminded of my love for you
in some small ways throughout your life.

My love is a legacy I leave to you.
I want you to know I wish
the very best for you always.
Being a part of your life has been
a blessing and a privilege.

♡ Dianne Cogar

*A*nd then there was one particularly poignant moment when I took a break from cookie baking to watch my oldest granddaughter playing in the backyard garden. She was wearing one of her mother's old dresses and when she stood under our arbor, I had to catch my breath. It was as if I was looking into a crystal ball, and there was my Izzy, twenty years from now on her wedding day. My eyes blurred with tears as I said a little prayer of thanks for the gift that is my granddaughters.

♡ Marcia Kester Doyle

*F*or every smile you bring
    to my heart,
for every moment we share
    making memories,
for every time you show me
just how special a grandchild you are,
I am reminded of how thankful I am
for the love that touches
my life so deeply.

♡ Susan Hickman Sater

I Am So Proud of You

I am so happy with the direction
that your life is taking you
You are unique and special
and I know that
your talents will give you
many paths to choose from
in the future
Always keep your many interests —
they will allow your mind
to remain energized
Always keep your positive outlook —
it will give you the strength to
accomplish great things
Always keep your determination —
it will give you the ability
to succeed in meeting your goals
Always keep your excitement
about whatever you do —
it will help you to have fun

Always keep your sense of humor —
it will allow you to
make mistakes and learn from them
Always keep your confidence —
it will allow you to take risks
and not be afraid of failure
Always keep your sensitivity —
it will help you to understand
and do something about
injustices in the world
Always remember that
I am more proud of you
than ever before

♡ Susan Polis Schutz

You're in My Heart Forever

You're the star in my sky. You're an angel from head to toe. I know you came straight from heaven. You're the memories I cherish and a dream come true. No wonder I love you as much as I do.

You're extraordinary. You're a treasure. You're all my wishes coming true and every prayer answered. Joy comes so easily to my world whenever you're around. You're full of fun times and you are so fun to be with. You're the best there is and the best there'll ever be. You're my second chance to be a kid again too.

You're amazing — and the sweetest thing I've ever known. You're all I'll ever need wrapped up in just one smile. You're the moments that make my heart melt; you're love and light and laughter by the heartful. You're a thousand gifts to me, and you brighten my life just like the sun brightens the world. You're in my heart forever.

♡ Linda E. Knight

I Love You, Granddaughter

You have grown from a precious and sweet child to a wonderful and kind adult, and my heart beams with pride to be your grandmother. I am so proud of all your accomplishments and deeply thankful for all that we share.